A Teaching Guide to

Where the Red Fern Grows

by Mary F. Spicer

Illustration by Kathy Kifer and Dahna Solar

Dedicated to
Wendel Z. (Sam) Hall
1938-1994
A teacher's teacher—always a source of inspiration
and encouragement to me.

Where the Red Fern Grows
A Bantam Book
Published by arrangement with Doubleday
New York, New York 10036

Published by:
Garlic Press
100 Hillview Lane #2
Eugene, OR 97408

ISBN 0-931993-77-6
Order Number GP-077

Table of Contents

The Discovering Literature Series is designed to develop a student's appreciation for good literature and to improve reading comprehension. While many skills reinforce a student's ability to comprehend what he or she reads (sequencing, cause and effect, finding details, using context clues), two skills are vital. They are: discerning **main ideas** and **summarizing** text. Students who can master these two essential skills develop into sophisticated readers.

The following discussion details the various elements that structure this Series.

About Chapter Organization

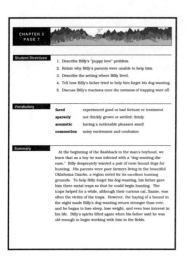

Sample: Chapter 2
with Student Directives,
Chapter Vocabulary, and
Chapter Summary

Each chapter analysis is organized into three basic elements: **Student Directives**, **Chapter Vocabulary**, and **Chapter Summary**. Student Directives and Chapter Vocabulary need to be displayed on the board or on an overhead projector after each chapter is read. Students copy the Chapter Vocabulary and write their own summaries following the Student Directives.

The **Student Directives** contain the main ideas in each chapter. They provide the students, working individually or in groups, with a framework for developing their summaries. Student Directives can also be used as group discussion topics.

The **Chapter Vocabulary** includes definitions of key words from each chapter. To save time, students need only to copy, not look up, definitions. Suggestions for teaching vocabulary to students are as follows:

1. Make and display flashcards with the words and definitions. Refer to vocabulary cards in daily review.
2. Have students write sentences individually, in groups, or as a class using the words in the story's context.
3. Give frequent quizzes before an actual test.
4. Have students make their own vocabulary crossword puzzles or word search puzzles.
5. Play 20 questions with vocabulary words.
6. Host a vocabulary bee where the students give definitions for the word rather than spelling it.

A **Chapter Summary** for each chapter is included for teacher use and knowledge. Some students may initially need to copy the summaries in order to feel comfortable writing their own subsequent ones. Other students can use the completed summaries as a comparison to guide their own work. Summary

Sample:
Blackline Master

writing provides an opportunity to polish student composition skills, in addition to reading skills.

The **blackline master**, *Chapter Summary & Vocabulary*, is provided on page 62. It can be duplicated for student use. Teachers can also use it to make transparencies for displaying Student Directives and Chapter Vocabulary.

In addition, teachers may opt to have students make folders to house their Chapter Summary & Vocabulary sheets. A sample cover sheet (see page 63) for student embellishments has been provided. Cover sheets can be laminated, if desired, and affixed to a manila (or other) folder.

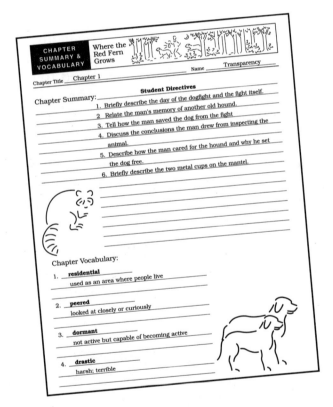

Sample Transparency:
Student Directives and Chapter Vocabulary

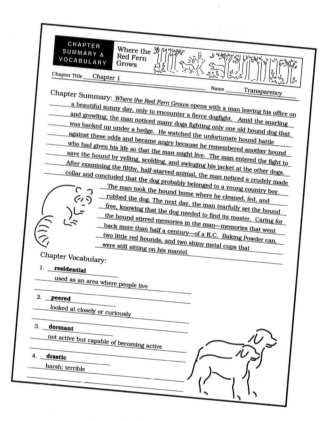

Sample Transparency:
Chapter Summary and Chapter Vocabulary

The above two samples serve to illustrate how the **blackline master**, *Chapter Summary & Vocabulary*, can be used as a transparency to focus student work. These transparencies are particularly effective for displaying Student Directives and Chapter Vocabulary. They are also effective for initially modeling how Chapter Summaries can be written.

About the Skill Pages

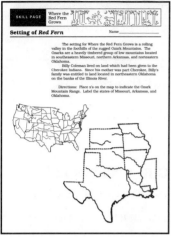

Sample: Skill Page

Skill Pages throughout the series have been developed to increase students' understanding of various literary elements and to reinforce vital reading skills. Since the entire series is devoted to reinforcing **main ideas** and **summarizing** skills, no further work has been provided on these skills. Depending upon each novel, Skill Pages reinforce various skills from among the following: **outlining**; **cause and effect**; **sequencing**; **character**, **setting**, **and plot development**; and **figurative language**. You will note that character development is based upon a values framework.

About the Tests

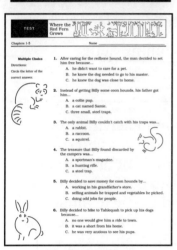

Sample: Test

At the end of each five-chapter block, a comprehensive open-book **Test** has been developed for your use. Each test includes reading comprehension, vocabulary, and short essays.

An Answer Key is provided at the back of the book for each Test.

The vocabulary portion of the Tests may be particularly difficult. You will probably want to give one or two vocabulary quizzes before administering each of the four Tests.

About the Writer's Forum

Sample: Writer's Forum

Suggestions for writing are presented under the **Writer's Forum** throughout this guide. You can choose from these suggestions or substitute your own creative-writing ideas.

Student Directives

1. Briefly describe the day of the dogfight and the fight itself.

2 Relate the man's memory of another old hound.

3. Tell how the man saved the dog from the fight.

4. Discuss the conclusions the man drew from inspecting the animal.

5. Describe how the man cared for the hound and why he set the dog free.

6. Briefly describe the two metal cups on the mantel.

Vocabulary

residential   used as an area where people live

peered   looked at closely or curiously

dormant   not active but capable of becoming active

drastic   harsh; terrible

Summary

Where the Red Fern Grows opens with a man leaving his office on a beautiful sunny day, only to encounter a fierce dog-fight. Amid the snarling and growling, the man noticed many dogs fighting only one old hound dog that was backed up under a hedge. He watched the unfortunate hound battle against these odds and became angry because he remembered another hound who had given his life so that the man might live. The man entered the fight to save the hound by yelling, scolding, and swinging his jacket at the other dogs. After examining the filthy, half-starved animal, the man noticed a crudely made collar and concluded that the dog probably belonged to a young country boy. The man took the hound home where he cleaned, fed, and rubbed the dog. The next day, the man tearfully set the hound free, knowing that the dog needed to find its master. Caring for the hound stirred memories in the man—memories that went back more than half a century—of a K.C. Baking Powder can, two little red hounds, and two shiny metal cups that were still sitting on his mantel.

Flashback Technique

A flashback is an interruption in a story by narration of some earlier episode. The flashback technique allows the author to open with a dramatic incident that captures the reader's imagination, compelling him or her to keep on reading. The man tells his own story in Chapter 2.

Student Directives

1. Describe Billy's "puppy love" problem.

2. Relate why Billy's parents were unable to help him.

3. Describe the setting where Billy lived.

4. Tell how Billy's father tried to help him forget his dog-wanting.

5. Discuss Billy's reactions once the newness of trapping wore off.

Vocabulary

fared   experienced good or bad fortune or treatment

sparsely   not thickly grown or settled; thinly

aromatic   having a noticeable pleasant smell

commotion   noisy excitement and confusion

Summary

At the beginning of the flashback to the man's boyhood, we learn that as a boy he was infected with a "dog-wanting disease." Billy desperately wanted a pair of coon hound dogs for hunting. His parents were poor farmers living in the beautiful Oklahoma Ozarks, a region noted for its excellent hunting grounds. To help Billy forget his dog-wanting, his father gave him three metal traps so that he could begin hunting. The traps helped for a while, although their curious cat, Samie, was often the victim of the traps. However, the baying of a hound in the night made Billy's dog-wanting return stronger than ever, and he began to lose sleep, lose weight, and even lose interest in his life. Billy's spirits lifted again when his father said he was old enough to begin working with him in the fields.

Setting of *Red Fern*, Page 1

Name_____

The setting of *Where the Red Fern Grows* is a rolling valley in the foothills of the rugged Ozark Mountains. The Ozarks are a heavily timbered group of low mountains located in southwestern Missouri, northern Arkansas, and northeastern Oklahoma.

Billy lived on land that had been given to the Cherokee Indians. Since his mother was part Cherokee, Billy's family was entitled to land located in northeastern Oklahoma on the banks of the Illinois River.

Directions:	Place X's on the map to indicate the Ozark Mountain Range. Label the states of Missouri, Arkansas, Oklahoma, Texas, Kansas, Mississippi, and Lousiana.

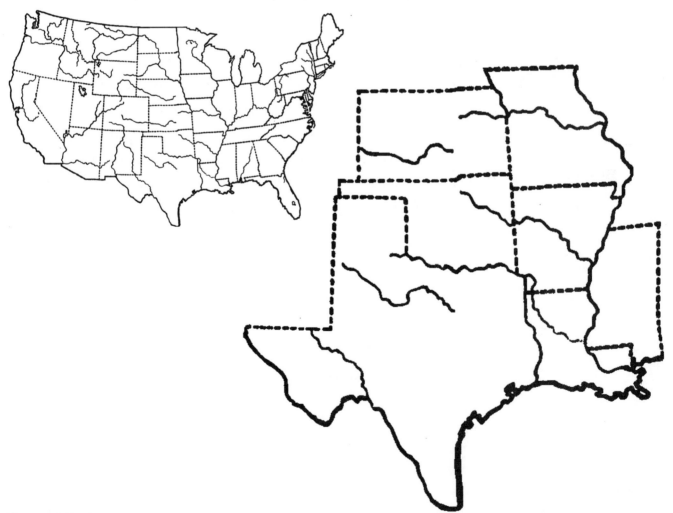

Setting of *Red Fern,* Page 2

Name_____

Directions: Write a cinquain poem about the Ozark Mountains. A cinquain is a five-line poem that follows a pattern. The pattern for cinquains follows, as do two examples.

Cinquain Pattern

Line 1:   One word that names the topic (noun).

Line 2:   Two words that describe the topic (adjectives).

Line 3:   Three action words that end in -ing (verbs).

Line 4:   Four-word phrase about the topic (phrase).

Line 5:   One word that relates to the topic (noun).

Cinquain Examples

Seacoast

Rhythmic, rocky

Glistening, rolling, crashing

Waves across the sand

Beaches

Football

Rough, aggressive

Running, throwing, tackling

Many bumps and bruises

Sport

Your Cinquain

Ozarks

_____   _____

_____ , _____ , _____

_____

_____

Student Directives

1. Describe the treasure Billy found at the fishermen's camp.

2. Tell about Billy's plan to save money for the coon hounds.

3. Discuss what Billy found to use as a bank.

4. Tell how long Billy worked to save for his hounds.

5. Describe his grandfather's reaction when Billy had saved enough money to order the hounds.

Vocabulary

festered   became painful or inflamed

mulled   thought about slowly and carefully

urgency   quality or state of needing immediate attention

dumbfounded amazed

Summary

Billy's dog-wanting never did leave him even when he was working with his Papa. One day while searching through the grounds where fishermen had recently camped, Billy discovered a great treasure for a poor country boy—a sportsman's magazine. While reading the "Dogs for Sale" section, Billy found an ad that took his breath away: "Registered redbone coon hound pups—twenty-five dollars each." After praying to God to help him get the hound pups, Billy devised a plan to earn the money himself. He would sell bait and vegetables to fishermen and sell the berries he picked and the animal skins from his trapping. While looking through the trash the next morning, Billy found a bank for his savings—an old K.C. Baking Powder can. Billy worked for two long years, saving his money until he had $50. When Billy asked his grandfather to order the pups from the magazine ad, his grandfather's eyes became moist. He realized how hard Billy had worked and sacrificed to save for the coon pups. As a special treat, Billy's grandfather gave him extra candy from his store, which Billy shared with his three younger sisters.

What Do You Think...

Name _____

About Running Away from Home?

Billy decided to leave home after his mama told him that he should be satisfied with his traps and that he was not to pester her about hound pups again. Billy packed peaches, corn bread, and a few onions, and set out on his own. He changed his mind, though, when he heard a timber wolf howling.

Has there ever been a time when you decided to run away from home? Did your plan succeed, or did you change your mind? Write about your experience.

_____

_____

_____

_____

_____

_____

_____

Continue writing on additional paper as needed.

About Wanting What You Can't Have?

Billy wanted a pair of coon pups so badly that he could think of nothing else. Have you ever wanted something so badly that it meant the world to you? Write about what you wanted and how you were able to resolve your problem.

_____

_____

_____

_____

_____

_____

Student Directives

1. Relate Billy's success in ordering his hounds.

2. Tell how Billy traveled to the Tahlequah depot.

3. Discuss Billy's reaction to the town and the townspeople's reaction to Billy.

Vocabulary

winced   moved away from, as in pain or from a blow

amends   something given or received to replace or fix a loss, injury, or damage

Summary

   Billy's letter from the dog kennel finally arrived, and Billy's grandfather ordered the coon hounds for him. His grandfather said that the price had dropped, so Billy got $10 back from his order. Billy's grandfather explained that he would be able to pick up his pups at the railroad depot in the nearby town of Tahlequah in two weeks. Billy was too anxious to wait for a ride to town, so he hiked twenty miles to get them himself. Since Billy had never been to town before, he marveled at the sights he saw. Using his $10 savings, Billy entered a store with a large window to purchase overalls for his papa, several yards of cloth for his mother and sisters, and a large sack of candy. He passed town children, who were playing in their schoolyard. They made fun of Billy, calling him "hillbilly." They thought Billy was odd because he didn't attend a regular school, he didn't wear shoes, and he lived in the hills. Even a little old lady who was working in her garden laughed at Billy as he slid down the long, blue pipe in the schoolyard. Billy just couldn't understand why the townspeople either stared at him or laughed at him.

Elements of a Narrative

When an author creates a novel, a movie, or a television script, he or she must carefully plan a text that includes three basic elements: characters, setting, and plot. Simply stated, *somebody* has to be *somewhere* doing *something* . The author's story has merit if the characters are believable, engaging, and well developed. The setting(s) must be accurately described so that the reader can create a mental picture of it in her or his own mind. Specific details are vital in the development of a narrative; details make the story "come alive" for the reader.

Possibly the most complex narrative element is the plot. To develop the plot, the author must carefully plan a sequence of events that will hold the reader's or viewer's interest throughout the book, movie, or TV show. The author must concentrate on only the important aspects of the story so that it doesn't drag on. Additionally, the events must present a problem that the central character must resolve—either happily or unhappily.

Throughout the introductory chapters or scenes, the author must make these elements—characters, setting, and plot—clear to the reader or viewer. Using the introductory chapters as a guide, complete the following "Elements of a Narrative Outline" for *Where the Red Fern Grows* .

Elements of a Narrative Outline

Name _____

Directions: Analyze the three basic elements of a narrative from your reading thus far in *Where the Red Fern Grows*. Complete the following outline for your analysis.

Main Character *(somebody)*   Describe Billy.

A. _____

_____

B. _____

_____

C. _____

_____

Setting *(somewhere)*   Describe the setting where the story unfolds.

A. Where: _____

_____

B. When: _____

_____

Plot *(something)*   From your reading so far, predict how the plot (as a series of events) will be developed.

A. _____

_____

B. _____

_____

C. _____

_____

D. _____

Student Directives

1. Describe the scene at the railroad depot.

2. Relate how a gang of boys attacked Billy.

3. Describe Billy's rescue.

4. Tell the characteristics that Billy noticed in each of his pups.

5. Relate how Billy saved his pups from the mountain lion.

Vocabulary

muster	to gather or summon
grit	fortitude; courage
ventured	took a risky or dangerous step

Summary

Billy was scared when he went to the depot, but ecstatic as he picked up his two pups. It was a case of love at first sight for both Billy and his dogs. On Billy's way out of town, he encountered the same rude stares and mocking laughter as he had when he entered town. A gang of boys began screaming and yelling at Billy. The leader of the gang stomped on Billy's foot and pulled the girl pup's ear. Billy began to fight the boys, but he was outnumbered, and they began to kick and beat him. Fortunately, Billy was rescued by the marshal, who was amazed by Billy's grit in saving for two years to get his pups and in hiking twenty miles to pick them up from the depot. Billy marveled at his two small pups. He noted the fearless boldness of the larger, stronger boy dog and the quick intelligence of the smaller, more delicate girl dog. Billy felt that he had the best of both worlds with his two pups. Camping out overnight in a cave, Billy and his pups were frightened by a screaming mountain lion that had apparently caught the scent of the pups. Billy finally frightened the mountain lion away by keeping the fire roaring and by whooping and throwing rocks down the mountain. The pups helped by bawling at the lion, and after a time, the lion left.

Getting Organized

Name _____

Billy noted distinct physical and personality differences between his two pups right away. Use the following chart to organize the differences between the pups. Refer to pages 43-44.

Boy Dog

Physical Characteristics

_____

_____

_____

Personality Characteristics

_____

_____

Girl Dog

Physical Characteristics

_____

_____

_____

Personality Characteristics

_____

_____

Billy saved for two years to buy his pups. Use the following chart to show how he achieved his goal. Refer to pages 19-20.

What Billy Sold

_____

_____

_____

_____

Examples of Prices

_____

_____

_____

_____

Methods Billy Used for Catching/Hunting/Picking

_____

_____

_____

_____

TEST

Where the
Red Fern
Grows

Chapters 1-5, Page 1

Name _____

Multiple Choice

Directions:

Circle the letter of the

correct answer.

1. After caring for the redbone hound, the man decided to set him free because...

    A. he didn't want to care for a pet.

    B. he knew the dog needed to go to his master.

    C. he knew the dog was close to home.

2. Instead of getting Billy some coon hounds, his father got him...

    A. a collie pup.

    B. a cat named Samie.

    C. three small steel traps.

3. The only animal Billy couldn't catch with his traps was...

    A. a rabbit.

    B. a raccoon.

    C. a squirrel.

4. The treasure that Billy found discarded by the campers was...

    A. a sportsman's magazine.

    B. a hunting rifle.

    C. a steel trap.

5. Billy decided to save money for coon hounds by...

    A. working in his grandfather's store.

    B. selling animals he trapped and vegetables he picked.

    C. doing odd jobs for people.

6. Billy decided to hike to Tahlequah to pick up his dogs because...

    A. no one would give him a ride to town.

    B. it was a short walk from his home.

    C. he was very anxious to see his pups.

7. Billy was impressed with the town because...

    A. the people were friendly.

    B. there was such a variety of goods in the store.

    C. he wanted to attend their school.

8. When the gang of boys was beating Billy, he was saved by...

    A. the marshal.

    B. the old ladies he had met when he first came into town.

    C. the stationmaster from the depot.

9. The marshal felt that Billy...

    A. shouldn't have started the fight by showing his pups.

    B. should have come to town with his father.

    C. showed a lot of grit by saving his money for two years to buy his pups.

10. Billy was able to save his pups from the mountain lion by...

    A. firing a shot from his rifle.

    B. keeping the fire going and throwing rocks.

    C. scaring the lion with a tree limb.

Vocabulary

Directions:

Fill in the blank with

the correct word.

dormant	winced	ventured
sparsely	amends	festered
aromatic	muster	mulled
	grit	

1. _____   to gather or summon

2. _____   took a risky or dangerous step

3. _____   something given or received to replace a loss, injury, or damage

4. _____ to move away from, as in pain or from a blow

5. _____ not thickly grown or settled; thinly

6. _____ became painful or inflamed

7. _____ not active but capable of activity

8. _____ having a noticeable, pleasant smell

9. _____ fortitude; courage

10. _____ thought about slowly and carefully

Essay Questions

Directions:

Answer in complete

sentences.

1. Why did Wilson Rawls, the author, open his novel with the flashback technique?

   _____

   _____

   _____

2. When the man saw the town dogs ganging up on the old coon hound, what memory did the redbone hound bring back?

   _____

   _____

   _____

3. After the marshal rescued Billy, he questioned him about the pups. When he heard Billy's story, he muttered, "There's not a one in that bunch with that kind of grit." What did the marshal mean?

   _____

   _____

   _____

Student Directives

1. Discuss Billy's thoughts on his way home from Tahlequah.

2. Tell how Billy got the names for his pups.

3. Discuss the family's reaction to the pups.

4. Review the reason why Billy's mother wanted to move the family to town.

5. Tell how Billy's faith helped him.

Vocabulary

querying	questioning
sober	marked by seriousness
hampering	impeding, hindering, holding back

Summary

After frightening away the mountain lion the previous night, Billy was eager to get on his way. He stopped at the campground where he had found the sportsman's magazine and thought about names for his pups. After discarding many possibilities, Billy finally settled on Old Dan and Little Ann—names he saw carved in the bark of a sycamore tree. Billy realized that getting his two pups was all part of a perfect puzzle. Although Billy was apprehensive about telling his parents about the pups, he received a joyful welcome home. His family was delighted with the pups and the gifts he had purchased in town. When Billy told his father that he didn't like the way he had been treated in town, he was surprised to learn that his parents had hopes of moving the family there. Billy's mother wanted her children to have the opportunity to see the world, to meet people, and to go to a regular school. The next evening, Billy told his mama that his faith in God had helped him realize his dream.

Student Directives

1. Tell why Billy now needed a coonskin.

2. Briefly describe his grandfather's suggestion for catching raccoons.

3. Discuss the killing of the raccoon and Papa's views on sportsmanship.

4. Describe Billy's methods for training his pups.

5. Relate how Old Dan differed from Little Ann during training.

Vocabulary

wiley (wily)   crafty; cunning

lope   a run with bounding steps

leverage   mechanical advantage or power gained by using a lever

Summary

Now that Billy had his hound pups, he desperately needed a coonskin so he could train them. When Billy was unable to trap a coon himself, he turned to his grandfather for help. His grandfather suggested a trap using a bit, a brace, and some nails, with a bright shiny piece of metal to serve as bait. Billy wasn't sure the trap would work, but he eventually caught a coon, and his papa had to club the captured coon to death. Since the coon had no chance of escape, Papa warned Billy not to use that kind of trap after this one time. During the training session with the pups, Old Dan would sometimes overrun a trail, but Little Ann would always figure it out. Billy worked hard training his pups, and he could hardly wait for hunting season to begin.

Student Directives

1. Briefly tell the differing reactions Billy's mama and papa had to his coon hunting.

2. Briefly describe the raccoon's tricks on Billy's first night of coon hunting.

3. Discuss Billy's reaction when his pups finally treed the coon.

4. Relate Billy's decision to keep his bargain with his dogs.

Vocabulary

pursed   contracted into folds or wrinkles; puckered

raved   talked wildly and excitedly

Summary

   Billy's mama and papa differed in their reactions to coon hunting. Papa completely understood Billy's desire to capture raccoons, but Mama disliked hunting and worried about Billy's safety. On the first night of hunting, Old Dan and Little Ann were tricked by a raccoon leaping into the water and crossing the river. Remembering her training, Little Ann eventually picked up the trail with Old Dan eagerly joining her. After climbing a water oak and disappearing for a while, the wily raccoon again fooled the dogs. Billy's dogs wouldn't give up their search, so the frightened raccoon decided to head for the mountains and then back again. When his pups finally treed their first raccoon, Billy was speechless because the tree was huge; it was a sycamore he had named "the big tree." At first Billy gave up any hope of ever being able to chop down the gigantic tree, but on seeing the disappointment in his pups' eyes, he remembered his bargain with his dogs and began chopping at the huge tree.

Identifying Characters, Page 1

Name_____

Directions: Characters from *Where the Red Fern Grows* are listed below. Fill in the correct character's name next to their appropriate quote. Names can be used more than once.

Billy   Papa   Mama   Grandpa   Boy in Tahlequah

Marshal   Billy's Sister

_____ 1. "Papa, I don't want an old collie dog. I want hounds—coon hounds—and I want two of them." (p. 8)

_____ 2. "You're going to have to do something. I never saw a boy grieve like that. It's not right, not right at all." (p. 9)

_____ 3. "I offered to get him a dog, but he doesn't want just any kind of dog. He wants hounds, and they cost money." (p. 10)

_____ 4. "Aw, there's nothing wrong with him. It's just because he's been cooped up all winter. A boy needs sunshine, and exercise. He's almost eleven now, and I'm going to let him help me in the fields this summer. That will put the muscles back on him." (p. 15)

_____ 5. "Would you like to buy some crawfish or minnows? Maybe you'd like some fresh vegetables or roasting ears." (p. 20- 21)

_____ 6. "Well, Son, it's your money. You worked for it, and you worked hard. You got it honestly, and you want some dogs. We're going to get those dogs." (p. 23)

_____ 7. "You go to school at home, and don't know what grade you're in. Who teaches you?" (p. 32)

_____ 8. "Those kids are pretty tough, son, but they're really not bad. They'll grow up some day." (p. 41)

_____ 9. "...and to beat it all, the boys jumped on me and knocked me down in the dirt. If it hadn't been for the marshal, I would have taken a beating." (p. 51)

_____ 10. "I'll pray every day and night for that day to come. I don't want you children to grow up without an education, not even knowing what a bottle of soda pop is, or ever seeing the inside of a schoolhouse." (p. 52)

_____ 11. "He needs a whipping, that's what he needs, scaring Mama that way." (p. 63)

_____ 12. "I want you to take a hammer and pull the nails from every one of those traps... I don't think this is very sportsmanlike. The coon doesn't have a chance." (p. 65-66)

_____ 13. "It's all right with me, but women are a little different than men. They worry more." (p. 70)

_____ 14. "I've waited almost three years for this night, and it hasn't been easy. I've taught you everything I know and I want you to do your best." (p. 70)

_____ 15. "Billy, I don't approve of this hunting, but it looks like I can't say no; not after all you've been through, getting your dogs, and all that training." (p. 70)

Student Directives

1. Describe Grandpa's trick to keep the raccoon treed.

2. Tell what "the backtracking trick" means.

3. Relate how Billy's dogs joined in the effort to keep the coon treed.

4. Discuss how Billy's faith in God gave him the strength to complete his task.

Vocabulary

limbered   loosened; made flexible; unstiffened

droning   making a dull, continued monotonous sound; humming; buzzing

resistance   the opposition by one thing, force, etc., to another

whiled   caused time to pass in some easy or pleasant manner

Summary

Billy spent the day chopping away at "the big tree." By evening he was tired and hungry, but his job wasn't even near completion. Billy's grandfather helped him make a scarecrow to trick the coon into thinking a real man was standing guard, giving Billy some time for a break. Grandpa explained that the coon had used "the backtracking trick" to fool Billy's pups. By climbing the water oak only about 15 or 20 feet before coming down in his same tracks, the wily raccoon had tricked the pups before Little Ann figured out the coon's strategy. Even with the scarecrow man standing guard, Billy's pups had spent the entire night guarding the treed coon. Although Billy's muscles were stiff and sore, he spent the next day chopping the huge tree. By late afternoon, exhausted and bleeding from many blisters and almost ready to give up, Billy knelt to pray for strength. Upon resuming his task, Billy heard the droning sound of a high wind that toppled the huge tree, and Billy knew his prayer had been answered.

Outlining, Page 1

Name _____

Outlining is an essential skill for organizing your thoughts and learning new material. Below is an article about the animal Billy Colman loved to hunt—the raccoon.

Read the article carefully. Then consult the Topics List to complete the outline. Some topics have been done for you. Remember that outlines are divided into main topics and sub-topics. Each indentation on the outline means that the topic listed directly above has been further divided into subtopics.

Raccoons

Raccoons are one of the most popular animals found in the wild. Because of their intelligence and adaptability, raccoons are a favorite animal with authors and have appeared in many stories and folktales.

Their physical appearance, as well as their behavior, makes raccoons appealing to many people. This grey or brown furry animal sports a black mask across its eyes, making it look a bit like a masked bandit. Its bushy tail, ringed with black markings, completes the picture of the mischievous woodland robber.

One particular habit makes raccoons seem almost human. In captivity, before eating their food, raccoons put their food in water and then take it out again. Rather than being concerned about washing their food, raccoons are thought to be making up for "missed behavior" in the wild. In their natural habitat, raccoons must paddle their front paws to catch their food in water. In captivity, raccoons are merely repeating behavior necessary for survival in the wild.

Another remarkable feature of the raccoon is its forepaws, which have five fingers. Looking somewhat like a small human hand, the raccoon's forepaw is able to manipulate objects that other animals cannot.

Raccoons have eating habits similar to humans. Raccoons are carnivores; thet eat frogs, crayfish, and insects. In addition to meat, raccoons also eat their share of plants—including farmers' crops.

Raccoons live in the woodlands, usually near water. Because many woods have been cleared, raccoons have sometimes been forced to move into the open country or suburbs, where they can become pests. The range across which raccoons can be found is broad—from Canada across the U.S. to Central America.

Outlining, Page 2

Name_____

Raccoons are as much at home in the water as they are on land. They are excellent swimmers, often evading hunters with this talent. Because raccoons are active at night, this is the time they are hunted.

Raccoons have been prized by hunters for many years because of their furry pelts, known as "coonskins." Some people also hunt raccoons because of the damage they do to crops.

Directions: An incomplete outline for "Raccoons" is given in the left column. Choose from the right column to complete the outline. Parts of the outline have been properly placed for you.

Raccoons

I. Popularity

    A. _____

    B. _____

    C. _____

II. Physical Appearance

    A. Black mask

       1. _____

       2. _____

    B. Grey or brown fur

    C. _____

       1. _____

       2. Ringed with black markings

Topics List
Choose from:

I.

    Appear in stories and folktales

    Intelligent and adaptable

    Favorite of authors

II.

    Tail

    Across its eyes

    Bushy

    Looks like bandit

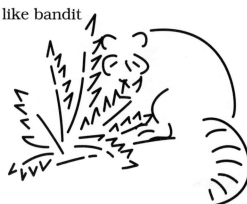

Outlining, Page 3

Name _____

III. Characteristics

    A. "Washing food"

        1. _____

        2. _____

    B.

        1. Five fingers

        2. _____

    C. Eating habits

        1. _____

        2. _____

IV. Habitat

    A. _____

    B. _____

    C. _____

V. Hunting Raccoons

    A. Done at night

    B. Reasons for hunting

        1. _____

        2. _____

III.

    Carnivores

    Done in captivity

    Forepaws

    Also eat plants

    Makes up for "missed behavior" in wild

    Highly manipulative

IV.

    Open country or suburbs

    Woodlands—near water

    Range—Canada to Central America

V.

    Damage to crops

    Coonskins

Student Directives

1. Discuss the benefits of Billy's coon hunting.

2. Tell how Billy enjoyed his Saturdays.

3. Describe some of Billy's unusual hunting experiences.

Vocabulary

nonchalantly   in a coolly unconcerned, indifferent manner

belligerent   warlike; aggressive

destined   predetermined; intended; fated

eerie   inspiring fear; weird, strange

Summary

Billy happily continued with his coon hunting, and as Grandpa had predicted, the price for coonskins jumped sky-high. Caring only about his dogs, Billy turned over all his earnings to his father. Billy especially enjoyed Saturdays at his grandfather's store, where all the coon hunters told whopping stories about their hunting experiences. Because of Old Dan's daring strength and Little Ann's keen intelligence, Billy's dogs had become expert hunters. Billy felt that his dogs made a perfect team. Little Ann, by a strange twist of fate, was destined never to become a mother. During one hunt, Billy's dogs were nearly fooled by a crafty coon who had climbed onto a branch hanging over the river. After chasing the coon down-river into a muskrat's den, Old Dan became trapped and could have died. Fortunately, Little Ann showed Billy the den's location, and with the help of a shovel, Billy was able to rescue Old Dan and bring him to safety. Another time, Old Dan climbed the inside of a hollow tree to trap a coon, and Billy had to stuff rocks into the tree's hollow to keep Old Dan from chasing the prey.

TEST	Where the Red Fern Grows

Chapters 6-10, Page 1   Name _____

Multiple Choice

Directions:

Circle the letter of the

correct answer.

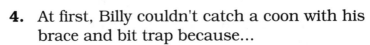

1. Billy decided on names for his pups by...

    A. asking his grandfather's advice.

    B. getting them off an old K.C. Baking Powder can.

    C. using names he saw carved into a tree.

2. When Billy arrived home with his pups, his parents...

    A. were relieved and happy to see him.

    B. were angry because Billy hadn't told them where he was going.

    C. didn't want him to keep the pups because they had cost too much money.

3. The bait Grandpa suggested using so Billy could trap his first coon was...

    A. a piece of raw meat.

    B. a piece of bright shiny tin.

    C. some horseshoe nails.

4. At first, Billy couldn't catch a coon with his brace and bit trap because...

    A. the coons were too smart for the trap.

    B. the coons didn't like Billy's bait.

    C. Billy had left too much scent around his traps.

5. Papa didn't want Billy to use the brace and bit trap after catching his first coon because...

    A. it wasn't very sportsmanlike.

    B. it was too time-consuming.

    C. it was too expensive.

6. Billy refused to let his father help him chop down "the big tree" because...

    A. Billy knew his father was needed on the farm.

    B. the tree was not difficult to chop.

    C. Billy had made a bargain with his dogs.

TEST

Where the
Red Fern
Grows

Chapters 6-10, Page 2

Name _____

7. When Billy's sister saw him chopping down the huge sycamore, she...

    A. was afraid that the tree might fall on Billy.

    B. thought Billy was crazy.

    C. offered to help him.

8. Grandpa's suggestion for guarding the treed coon was...

    A. to let Old Dan and Little Ann guard the tree while Billy rested.

    B. to take turns guarding the tree.

    C. to make a scarecrow man to trick the raccoon.

9. Grandpa's reaction to Billy cutting down the huge sycamore was...

    A. disgust because the tree was too good to waste.

    B. pride because the experience would give Billy determination and will power.

    C. laughter because the raccoon was so comical.

10. Billy's reaction to the coon hunters' whopping stories was...

    A. enjoyment because he liked swapping stories.

    B. anger because he felt his dogs were better hunters than theirs.

    C. disgust because he felt that the hunters lied.

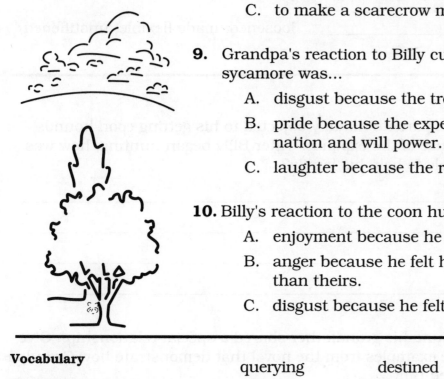

Vocabulary

Directions:

Fill in the blank with

the correct word.

querying	destined	belligerent
eerie	wily	resistance
limbered	lope	nonchalantly
	raved	

1. _____ inspiring fear; weird, strange

2. _____ a run with bounding steps

3. _____ the opposition by one thing, force, etc., to another

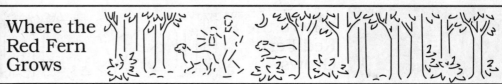
4. _____   warlike; aggressive

5. _____   questioning

6. _____   crafty; cunning

7. _____   talked wildly and excitedly

8. _____   in a coolly unconcerned, indifferent
                          manner

9. _____   predetermined; intended; fated

10. _____   loosened; made flexible; unstiffened

Essay Questions

Directions:

Answer in complete

sentences.

1. Billy's parents initially objected to his getting coon hounds
   because of the expense. After Billy began hunting, how was
   he able to help his family?

   _____

   _____

   _____

   _____

2. Billy and his grandfather shared a special relationship. Give
   three examples from the novel that demonstrate how Grandpa
   helped Billy.

   _____

   _____

   _____

   _____

   _____

   _____

Student Directives

1. Describe the fierce winter storm.

2. Relate the deadly trick that the raccoon played on Old Dan and Little Ann.

3. Review Billy's plan for saving Little Ann.

4. Discuss Billy's behavior after returning home.

Vocabulary

predicament dangerous or unpleasant situation

rile to make cross or angry; to irritate

eddy little whirlpool or circular current

plight dangerous or awkward situation

Summary

A fierce northern blizzard blew into the Ozark region where Billy lived, freezing, snowing, and blowing for five days. When the storm lifted, Billy took his dogs hunting even though the ice was slick and the night was dark. A wily raccoon played a deadly trick on Billy's dogs that night. Leading them to the river, the raccoon ran out onto the ice and jumped the trough to the other side. Old Dan was strong enough to make the leap, but Little Ann plunged into the icy river and was near death. Desperately, Billy tried to devise a plan to save her. After sobbing out a prayer, Billy heard a metallic sound, which gave him an idea. He took the handle off his lantern and bent it into a hook. He used his shoelaces to tie the wire to the end of a cane pole. Inch by inch, he waded into the water until he could snag Little Ann's collar. Afterwards, Billy started a fire and rubbed and massaged Little Ann back to life. Old Dan had whined frantically during his mate's plight. Now he helped Billy by licking Little Ann with his tongue. Billy decided not to tell his parents about Little Ann's accident, which left him sick in bed for three days afterward.

Student Directives

1. Review how Grandpa's bragging got Billy into trouble with the Pritchard boys.

2. Briefly describe the Pritchard family, Rubin, and Rainie.

3. Tell about the bet Grandpa made.

4. Briefly describe the hunt for the "ghost coon."

Vocabulary

leering   looking with a sidelong glance that indicates bad intentions.

begrudgingly in a reluctant manner, with ill will

maneuver   a skillful movement toward an object

Summary

Grandpa frequently bragged about Billy's exploits with his dogs. Because of his bragging, Billy became involved in a bet with the Pritchard boys. The Pritchards were a large family that no one liked. Rubin, two years older than Billy, was a large, husky boy with mean-looking eyes. Rainie, the youngest Pritchard boy, was about Billy's age and had the meanest disposition of anyone Billy had ever known. Billy's mother said that Rainie was mean because his brothers were always picking on him and beating him. The Pritchard boys challenged Billy and his grandfather to a bet that Billy's dogs couldn't tree the ghost coon. Grandpa put up the money. The following evening Billy met Rubin and Rainie at the designated spot, and the hunt began. The wily raccoon attempted to trick Billy's dogs by swimming upstream rather than downstream. Old Dan was more easily fooled by the raccoon, and attempted to find him in the submerged hollow of a tree. Searching carefully, Little Ann was able to pick up the ghost coon's trail. Crossing the river time after time, the ghost coon headed for the tree where he always disappeared.

Sequencing

Name _____

Event 1: Billy gets "dog-wanting disease."
_____

Event 2: _____
_____

Event 3: _____
_____

Event 4: _____
_____

Event 5: _____
_____

Event 6: The marshal saves Billy.
_____

Event 7: _____
_____

Event 8: _____
_____

Event 9: _____
_____

Event 10: Little Ann almost freezes.
_____

Event 11: _____
_____

Event 12: _____
_____

Directions:

Using the timeline provided, sequence the following events from Chapters 1-12. Three events have been done for you.

- Billy finds magazine.
- The marshal saves Billy.
- Billy gets "dog-wanting disease."
- Billy picks up pups.
- Billy sets steel traps.
- Billy outsmarts mountain lion.
- Grandpa brags about Billy's dogs.
- Billy begins saving.
- Billy chops "the big tree".
- Little Ann almost freezes.
- The Pritchards challenge Billy.
- Billy gives earnings to papa.

Student Directives

1. Discuss the trick the ghost coon played with the bur oak and the large gatepost.

2. Tell why Billy didn't want to kill the ghost coon.

3. Briefly describe the appearance of Old Blue and Billy's fight with Rubin.

4. Discuss Rubin's accident.

5. Tell about Billy's visit to Rubin's grave.

Vocabulary

taut	tight; firm
clambered	climbed with difficulty or in an awkward manner
protruding	thrusting or sticking out
stern	severe; forbidding; grim

Summary

The ghost coon had tricked hunters for many years by disappearing into the huge, squatty bur oak and running out on a long limb that hung over a hollow gatepost. After Billy discovered the coon's trick, he didn't have the heart to kill it. Billy figured the coon had lived a long time and deserved his freedom. Objecting violently, Rubin and Rainie were about to beat Billy when Old Blue, their mean ugly tick hound, appeared out of the darkness. As Rubin began to threaten and beat Billy, Old Blue challenged Old Dan to a fight. Although female dogs rarely enter a fight, Little Ann dug her jaws into Old Blue's throat to protect her mate. Together Billy's dogs were killing Old Blue. Grabbing Billy's ax, Rubin rushed to rescue his dog, but in his haste he accidentally tripped and fell on the ax. Terrified, Rainie ran from the scene. Billy, stunned and sickened by the sight before him, nevertheless responded to Rubin's plea to pull the protruding ax from his stomach. Rubin attempted to get up but gurgled and fell dead to the ground. Billy walked home to tell his parents the nightmarish story. Saddened and dazed by Rubin's death, Billy had no heart for hunting until he had placed a small wreath of flowers on Rubin's grave.

Figurative Language, Page 1

Name_____

Red Fern takes place in the heavily wooded Ozark foothills of Oklahoma. The people living there are country people who live close to the land. In writing *Where the Red Fern Grows*, Wilson Rawls captures the colorful language of these country people.

You will find that many of Rawls' expressions are similes. **Similes** are a type of figurative language that uses <u>like</u> or <u>as</u> to show similarities between two different things. (Example: gentle as a lamb)

Directions:
1. Read each figurative expression and discuss how its use enhanced the story. If the expression is a simile, write "simile" next to the expression.

2. Choose two of your favorite expressions and draw a cartoon for each. Be sure to use the expressions in your cartoon.

_____ 1. "The land was rich, black, and fertile. Papa said it would grow hair on a crosscut saw." (p. 8)

_____ 2. "His tail was as big as a wet corncob and every hair on his small body was sticking straight up." (p. 11)

_____ 3. "My straw-colored hair was long and shaggy, and was brushed out like a corn tassle that had been hit by a wind." (p. 29)

_____ 4. "I stuck out my tongue. It was as red as pokeberry juice..." (p. 29)

_____ 5. "When the words finally came out they sounded like the squeaky old pulley on our well when Mama drew up a bucket of water." (p. 36)

_____ 6. "I knew the pups were mine, all mine, yet I couldn't move. My heart started acting like a drunk grasshopper." (p. 37)

Figurative Language, Page 2

Name_____

_____ 7. "A sick look came over his face. Bending over, croaking like
a bullfrog that had been caught by a water moccasin,
he started going around in a circle." (p. 40)

_____ 8. "The sound seemed to be all around us. It screamed its way
into the cave and rang like a blacksmith's anvil against the
rock walls." (p. 45)

_____ 9. "With hog lard I greased my boots until they were as soft as a
hummingbird's nest." (p. 69)

_____ 10. "White sheets of water, knocked high in the moonlight by his
churning feet, gleamed like thousands of tiny white stars." (p. 74)

_____ 11. "His friendly old face was as red as a turkey gobbler's
wattle." (p. 126)

Cartoons

Simile Number _____   Simile Number _____

Student Directives

1. Discuss Grandpa's reaction to Rubin's death.

2. Tell about Grandpa's plan to enter the championship coon hunt.

3. Review Papa's reasons for not wanting to attend.

4. Briefly describe the preparation for the trip.

Vocabulary

jubilant	joyful and triumphant
gloated	looked upon with excessive satisfaction
sulking	being silently resentful; ill-humored; sullen
fleeting	passing rapidly

Summary

Soon after Rubin's death, Billy received a message that his grandfather wanted to see him. Dreading the prospect of explaining the tragedy over again, Billy reluctantly went to his grandfather's store. Grandpa felt responsible for Rubin's death and asked Billy to forget that it had ever happened. On a brighter note, Grandpa told Billy about the championship coon hunt in which he had entered Old Dan and Little Ann. After explaining the eligibility requirements to Billy, Grandpa said he had paid the entry fees and told Billy about the gold cup for the winner. On his way home, Billy felt that he was the luckiest boy in the world. Grandpa and Billy wanted Papa to go along on the trip. Papa reluctantly agreed to go, although he was worried about his wife's pregnancy and the farm. After promising the gold cup to his little sister if he won, Billy prepared for their trip. On the morning of their departure, Billy noticed the ax in the back of the wagon. Grandpa had kept it after Rubin's death. Billy agreed with Grandpa that it was a good ax and they shouldn't throw it away.

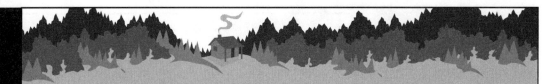

Student Directives

1. Discuss the relationship between Old Dan and Little Ann.

2. Briefly describe the contest campgrounds.

3. Review how Billy prepared Little Ann for the best-looking hound contest, and describe the outcome of the contest.

4. Discuss briefly the preparations for the coon hunt.

Vocabulary

domain   territory; empire

impulsively   acting suddenly without conscious thought

Summary

While camping along the way to the contest, Grandpa was amazed that Billy's dogs would wait for each other to begin eating. Papa also told how the dogs would share food with each other. Once they arrived at the campsite for the contest, Billy marveled at the size of it and the number of hunting dogs. He saw many types of dogs with slick, glossy coats and brass-studded collars. After selecting Little Ann to enter the contest for the best looking hound, Billy found he had no grooming brushes, so he impulsively reached for Grandpa's hair set and got some homemade butter to groom her. Despite Billy's fears that Little Ann was too small to win, she took first place and won a silver cup. After Little Ann's win, Billy learned the rules for the coon hunt and the process for eliminating the hunters who could not tree a coon. The contest would take several nights, and the hunters had to catch a coon, skin it, and turn the hide over to the judges. Billy and Grandpa restlessly waited for the fourth night, when it would be their turn to compete.

Cause and Effect

Name _____

Directions: On the left is list of causes. On the right is a list of effects. Match the correct effect with its cause by placing the correct letter in the blank.

A **Cause** produces a result.	An **Effect** results from a cause.
1. In order to get her children a good education, ____	A. Billy felt he had to chop down "the big tree" by himself.
2. So that Billy could train his pups to hunt coons, ____	B. he entered them in a championship coon hunt.
3. Because Little Ann was smart and careful, ____	C. they challenged Billy to a bet.
4. In order to keep his bargain with his dogs, ____	D. he jumped into the freezing water to save her.
5. Because coonskin coats were becoming a big fad back East, ____	E. Mama wanted to move to town.
6. When Billy saw that Little Ann was drowning, ____	F. Rainie Pritchard was a very mean boy.
7. Since his older brothers picked on him and beat him, ____	G. he needed a coonskin for their training sessions.
8. Because the Pritchard boys didn't believe the stories about Billy's dogs, ____	H. Old Dan wouldn't start eating until Little Ann received her share.
9. Grandpa thought Billy's dogs were superior hunters, so ____	I. she never overran a trail.
10. Because Billy's dogs shared everything they did, ____	J. Billy started making a lot of money selling coonskins.

TEST

Where the
Red Fern
Grows

Chapters 11-15, Page 1

Name _____

Multiple Choice

Directions:

Circle the letter of the

correct answer.

1. When Billy took his dogs hunting after the fierce winter storm, Little Ann...

    A. got buried in a huge snowdrift.

    B. almost drowned in the icy river.

    C. succeeded in treeing a coon.

2. The Pritchard family was...

    A. well liked by other families who lived in the Ozark foothills.

    B. a prosperous family that lived in town.

    C. a mean group that was always in trouble with the law.

3. The Pritchard boys wanted to bet Billy that...

    A. their dog could tree the ghost coon.

    B. Billy's dog couldn't tree the ghost coon.

    C. their dog could outrace Billy's dogs.

4. With regard to coon hunting, Little Ann...

    A. never brawled treed until she was sure she had the coon.

    B. was a better swimmer than Old Dan.

    C. always followed Old Dan's lead.

5. The ghost coon got its name from...

    A. the fact that it was smokey-colored.

    B. his fierce, frightening appearance.

    C. the way he seemed to disappear into a tree.

6. To enter the championship coon hunt, registrants had to...

    A. pay a $100 entry fee and write many letters.

    B. pay a fee and send the dogs' registration papers with the dogs' hunting record.

    C. personally know the organizers of the hunt.

7. Before leaving for the championship hunt, Billy promised the winning gold cup to his...

    A. mother.

    B. litter sister.

    C. grandfather.

8. The mountain superstition regarding the screeching of two owls meant that...

    A. a person hearing it would experience bad luck.

    B. a person hearing it would experience good luck.

    C. a storm was brewing.

9. Billy was apprehensive about entering his dogs in the championship hunt because...

    A. they did not have fancy collars and leashes.

    B. their hunting record was not as good as other dogs.

    C. they were small.

10. During each night of the hunt, teams were eliminated if...

    A. they used a gun to shoot the raccoon.

    B. they failed to capture and skin a coon.

    C. they went out of bounds.

Vocabulary

Directions:

Fill in the blank with the correct word.

plight	leering	jubilant
begrudgingly	taut	gloated
rile	clambered	fleeting
	stern	

1. _____   in a reluctant manner; with ill will

2. _____   joyful and triumphant

3. _____   climbed with difficulty or in an awkward manner

4. _____   looked upon with excessive satisfaction

5. _____   to make cross or angry; to irritate

6. _____   passing rapidly

7. _____   a dangerous or awkward situation

8. _____   looking slyly with bad intentions

9. _____   tight; firm

10. _____   severe; forbidding; grim

Essay Questions

Directions:

Answer in complete

sentences.

1. Billy Colman was a courageous boy who sometimes liked to
take chances. Give two examples from the novel where Billy
took chances that he didn't have to take.

_____

_____

_____

_____

_____

_____

2. Throughout the novel, Billy and his family demonstrate a high
sense of responsibility for their own actions. Give any two
examples from the novel that show this sense of responsibility.

_____

_____

_____

_____

_____

_____

Student Directives

1. Briefly discuss Billy's first two coons of the hunt.

2. Discuss the judge's concern about the third coon.

3. Review the run off of the winning teams.

4. Tell about getting the coon on elimination night.

Vocabulary

riffle   stretch of shallow, rapid, or choppy water

faltered   wavered; lost confidence; became unsteady

Summary

When the night of Billy's hunt came, he and the other hunters tried to get away from the already-hunted territory. Old Dan and Little Ann knew that this hunt was special, and they treed two coons in the early part of the night. Billy, Papa, Grandpa, and the judge spent all night hunting but after three o'clock, they began to fear that they wouldn't get the necessary third coon. Just as the judge was ready to quit, Old Dan opened on a coon's trail, and the hunt was on again. The wily raccoon tricked Billy's dogs, though, and daylight emerged. Finally, Little Ann bawled treed, and Old Dan rushed to help her. Amazed by the dog's hunting ability, the judge told Billy that he had tied with the leading teams. Of the three sets of dogs eligible for the run off, only the winner would take home a gold cup. On the final evening of the hunt, Papa's decision to hunt in the swamps was correct because Billy's dogs treed a coon quickly. After a rigorous struggle with the old coon in the water, Old Dan and Little Ann were again successful. The judge marveled at the way Billy's dogs cared for each other's wounds once the hunt had ended.

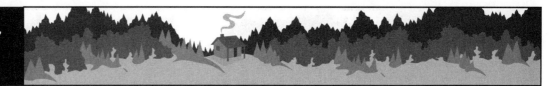

Student Directives

1. Describe the men's reaction to the storm.

2. Tell why Billy wanted to continue the hunt.

3. Discuss Grandpa's accident.

4. Tell about Old Dan's and Little Ann's perseverance in hunting the coons.

5. Discuss how Billy helped Grandpa's ankle.

Vocabulary

trudged   wearily walked or tramped

avail   advantage; use or help

Summary

While Billy, Papa, Grandpa, and the judge were coon hunting on the last night of the championship, a winter storm arrived bringing freezing sleet. The men, apprehensive about getting lost in the fierce storm, wanted to return to camp. Billy pleaded with them to stay in the woods until he had found his dogs. With Billy leading, the men trudged on through the icy sleet and howling winds. Papa fired his gun to signal Little Ann to return. She returned and began leading the group through the freezing storm to Old Dan. Billy found Old Dan half-frozen in a deep gully. As soon as he scraped the icy sleet from the dog's body, Old Dan ran to where he had treed a raccoon and howled. In all of the confusion, the men had not realized that Grandpa was no longer with them. Billy couldn't hold back the tears. Instinctively realizing the cause of Billy's sorrow, Little Ann led the group to where Grandpa had fallen after injuring his ankle. The men carried Grandpa to a shelter. Resuming the hunt, Papa felled the tree where Old Dan still howled. Everyone was surprised to find that Billy's dogs had treed not one but three coons in the hollow tree. Each dog made a kill and then chased the third coon into the freezing weather. Billy, still worried about his dogs, spent the entire night warming coonskins to soothe Grandpa's injured ankle.

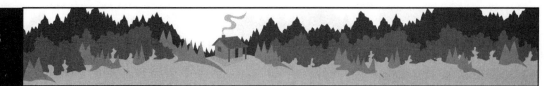

Student Directives

1. Briefly discuss the hunters' fear about Billy's group.

2. Discuss what happened to Billy's dogs during the night of the storm.

3. Tell about the championship win.

4. Describe the reaction of Billy's family to his win.

Vocabulary

defiant   full of boldness; challenging

awed   influenced by fear or respect

verge (n)   the edge, brink, or margin of something

allotted   divided up or distributed by lot

Summary

The hunters searched all night for Billy's group. They had become worried when the other team members who had separated from Billy's group returned to camp around midnight. Without realizing what he was saying, one of the hunters told Billy that his dogs had treed a coon and were frozen solid. Thinking the dogs had frozen to death, Billy momentarily passed out. Billy's dogs had followed the raccoon into the river and their wet fur had become frozen when they came out. To keep from freezing to death, the dogs had run all night around the tree where the coon was hiding. After finding the dogs, a fire was built to warm the dogs gradually. Once thawed, Old Dan and Little Ann killed the final coon—the one that was needed to win the championship. Grandpa was in pain from his sprained foot, but he stayed at the campground until he had seen the gold cup awarded to Billy. Billy was so moved by the joy of winning the gold cup and over $300 collected by the hunters that he even cried a little. Upon returning home, Billy's mother and sisters could scarcely believe his dogs had won two cups, the silver and gold. When Billy gave his mother the award money, she knew that her prayers had been answered.

Student Directives

1. Briefly describe the fight Billy and his dogs had with the mountain lion.

2. Discuss how Billy and his family attempted to save Old Dan.

3. Briefly describe Old Dan's and Little Ann's deaths and Billy's reaction.

4. Review the good that had come from Billy's dogs.

Vocabulary

predatory   preying on other animals

lithe   easily bent; flexible; limber

probed   searched

Summary

Billy resumed hunting with his dogs after winning the gold cup. One night, noticing that his dogs were behaving strangely, Billy realized that Old Dan had treed the devil cat of the Ozarks, the mountain lion. Due to his fighting nature, Old Dan refused to back off, and the angry cat sprang from its treetop perch to attack Old Dan. Little Ann rushed in to help her mate, and Billy began attacking with his ax. During the fight, Billy lost his footing and slipped. He would most certainly have been killed had his two dogs not jumped as one into the open jaws of the fierce mountain lion. Old Dan, having received terrible wounds to each side of his ribs, was bleeding profusely. Billy devised a mud pack to stop the bleeding. Little Ann's wounds were not so serious. After wrapping Old Dan in his sheepskin coat, Billy carried his beloved dog home where Mama doctored him by cleaning his entrails and stitching his wounds, but Old Dan's wounds were severe. He died that night. Grief-stricken, Billy made a coffin and buried Old Dan in a beautiful spot overlooking the countryside. After Old Dan's death, Little Ann stopped eating and lost her will to live. With her dying breath, she dragged herself to Old Dan's grave where she too died. Losing both of his dogs, Billy questioned God's providence. Papa felt that some good had emerged from the sorrow. Because of the dogs, the family had enough money to move to town where the children could get a good education. Also, with the dogs gone, Billy would not be separated from his family when the time came to move.

Student Directives

1. Discuss Billy's moving day.

2. Tell the legend of the red fern.

3. Relate how the legend helped Billy cope with his loss.

Summary

When moving day arrived, Billy's family, happy and joking, placed their belongings into their wagon. The glow in Mama's eyes made Billy feel good, and Billy noticed that Papa didn't have that whipped look on his face anymore. Before departing, Billy went to say good-bye to his dogs. Approaching the spot, Billy couldn't believe what he saw. Arching over the two graves was a beautiful red fern. According to Indian legend, a boy and girl had become lost in a blizzard and died. Their frozen bodies were discovered the following spring with a beautiful red fern growing between them. The Indians believed that only an angel could plant the seeds of a red fern. Once planted, red ferns never died; where a red fern grew, the spot was sacred. Billy, remembering the meaning of the legend, called to his family to see his discovery. Mama, staring unbelievingly, said she'd wanted to see a red fern all of her life. Papa felt that the red fern was God's way of helping Billy understand why his dogs had died. Feeling differently after seeing the red fern, Billy didn't hurt anymore. Even when Billy had grown to manhood, he never forgot his boyhood home in the Ozarks, his two faithful dogs, and the beautiful legend of the red fern.

Character Development

Billy Colman was a remarkable young boy. Despite coming from a poor family that eked out its living by farming, Billy set high goals for himself. When his parents were unable to help him reach his goal, Billy searched his own heart to come up with a solution to his problem. Believing that "God helps those who help themselves," Billy saved every cent he could earn for two years. At the end of that time, Billy had saved $50.00— enough to buy the two coon pups he had wanted for so long.

Wilson Rawls masterfully develops Billy's character through Billy's thoughts, conversations, and actions. Without his unshakeable faith in God and in himself, Billy would not have been able to pursue his dream for two long years.

Good literature, like *Where the Red Fern Grows*, serves not only to entertain and educate us, but also to enrich us spiritually. In analyzing Billy's character, not only do we learn about his character development, but we are also given examples of how we can strive to conduct our own lives. Like Billy Colman, it is important for us to develop our own strength of character.

The Discovering Literature Series focuses on ten character virtues:

Responsibility	Friendship
Courage	Persistence
Compassion	Hard Work
Loyalty	Self-discipline
Honesty	Faith

The following pages highlight these character virtues. Using examples from your reading, tell how Billy Colman embodies these virtues.

Character Development, Page 1

Name _____

Directions: Billy Colman portrays a strong, responsible character in *Where the Red Fern Grows*. Give examples from the novel to illustrate the virtues listed below.

Responsibility

_____

_____

_____

_____

_____

Courage

_____

_____

_____

_____

_____

Compassion

_____

_____

_____

_____

_____

Persistence

_____

_____

_____

_____

_____

_____

Character Development, Page 2

Name_____

Hard Work

_____

_____

_____

_____

_____

Faith

_____

_____

_____

_____

_____

Can you think of other qualities that Billy possessed? Give examples.

_____   _____

_____

_____

_____   _____

_____

_____

Which of Billy's virtues would you like to imitate? Why?

_____

_____

_____

_____

_____

_____

Plot Development

Authors must plan for three major elements—characters, setting, plot—when creating a story. Of the three narrative elements, plot is usually the most difficult to develop.

In every well-developed plot, the central character has a problem, or conflict, to overcome. The central problem can be a conflict between two people, between a character and the society in which she or he lives, between a character and nature, or it could even be a conflict within the main character. Whatever the conflict, the main character works through his or her problem throughout the novel or script. In doing so, the main character encounters a series of minor problems, or difficulties; however, these are all directed toward resolving the major conflict.

The structure of a plot can be compared to climbing a mountain. At the base of the mountain, the reader is introduced to the main characters and to the setting. The story develops and the reader is presented with a major problem to be overcome. All the while, the reader is steadily climbing the mountain until he or she reaches the peak, where the action reaches a high point or climax. As soon as the climax has been reached, the action falls rapidly—just as a mountain climber would when rushing down the back side of a mountain. Once the action falls, the reader sees the central character resolve her or his problem.

The Plot Organization Map graphically illustrates how the plot is developed. Using the Rising Action topics and Falling Action topics, complete the Plot Organization Map. Plot the events sequentially. Then fill in the characters, setting, problem, and resolution.

Duplicate the Plot Organization Map on oversize paper for ease of student use.

Rising Action

- Grandpa sends for pups.
- Dogs nearly freeze on hunt.
- Billy begs for pups.
- Rubin falls on Billy's ax.
- Billy works for pups.
- Billy's dogs win cups.
- Billy goes to town.
- Devil cat slashes Old Dan.
- Billy trains pups.
- Billy gives Mama over $300.

Falling Action

- Old Dan dies from wounds.
- Little Ann dies from grief.

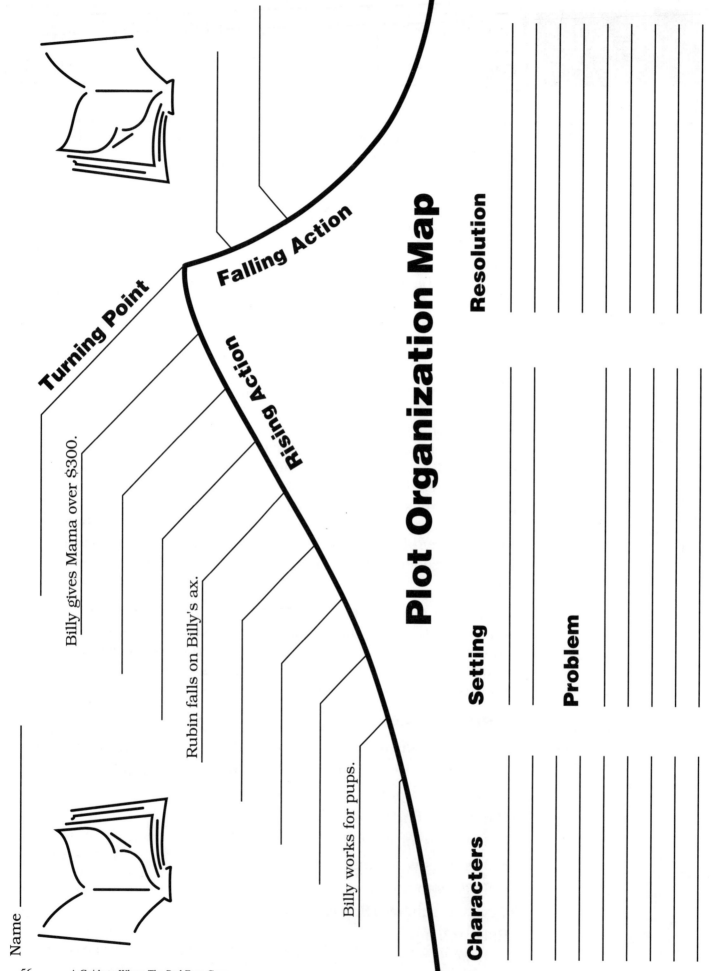

Plot Organization Map

Turning Point

Billy gives Mama over $300.

Falling Action

Rising Action

Rubin falls on Billy's ax.

Billy works for pups.

Resolution

Setting

Problem

Characters

WRITER'S FORUM	Where the Red Fern Grows

Name _____

Directions: Wilson Rawls suggests a number of thought-provoking topics in *Where the Red Fern Grows*. Choose one of the topics listed below, and develop it by using examples and details from your own experiences.

1. Throughout the novel, we read about Billy's strong relationship with his grandfather. When Billy feels that he can confide in no one else, he can always turn to his grandfather for understanding and help. Do you have a favorite grandparent or elderly person in your life—one who seems to understand you when no one else does? Write about a time when your favorite older person helped you with a problem.

2. After working hard to save for his pups, Billy did a masterful job of training them as well. Have you ever been responsible for training a puppy? Write about some of the problems you encountered with the training and how you eventually overcame them.

3. Throughout the novel, Billy unfailingly thinks of others. When his grandfather gave him extra candy, Billy always remembered to share some with his sisters. When Billy went to town to pick up his dogs, he used the extra $10 to purchase gifts for his family. Do you know someone who is thoughtful and generous like Billy was? Describe that person, giving several examples of their generosity.

4. Billy sometimes kept secrets from his parents. While he was saving money to buy his pups, Billy kept his secret to himself even though his poor family could have used the money he earned. When Billy got into trouble saving Little Ann from the freezing waters of the river, he kept that secret from his parents as well. Do you think that Billy was right to keep secrets from his parents, or should he have told them? Did keeping a secret ever get you in trouble? Explain how your situation worked out.

5. Billy's father had very strong feelings about the value of sportsmanship—even when it came to hunting raccoons. We read in Chapter 7 that Billy caught his first coon with a brace and bit trap. After catching that first coon, which Billy needed to train his pups, Papa made Billy dismantle the rest of his traps because "the coon doesn't have a chance." Write about your definition of sportsmanship. Be sure to give examples of sportsmanlike behavior from your own experiences.

6. Billy encountered some problems with bullies in *Where the Red Fern Grows*. He was attacked in town by a group of boys who teased and mocked him. Another time, while Billy was out hunting the ghost coon with the Pritchard brothers, Billy was attacked by Rubin. Have you ever experienced a problem with bullies? Write about an experience and tell how the situation was finally resolved.

7. The judges at the championship hunt were amazed by Billy's dogs. Not only did his dogs do everything together, including eating, but they also seemed to be able to read Billy's mind about hunting. Have you ever had a pet whose unusual behavior amazed people? Write about your pet and give examples of its unusual behavior.

8. Billy endured more grief than he thought he could stand when both of his dogs died. Have you ever experienced the loss of a beloved pet? Write about how you were able to deal with your loss.

9. At the end of the novel, we read that Billy's father firmly believed that some good could come out of tragedy. If Billy's dogs had not earned the championship money, Billy's family could never have moved to town. Also, if Billy's dogs had lived, he would have had to stay with his grandfather while the rest of his family moved. Have you ever experienced a time when some good came out of a bad situation? Write about that time and explain the positive results.

Multiple Choice

Directions:

Circle the letter of the

correct answer.

1. When daylight dawned on the night of the championship hunt, Billy and the men were worried because...

    A. the rules said hunting ended when daylight appeared.

    B. it was hard to keep a coon treed in the daylight.

    C. raccoons sleep during the day.

2. On the final night of the championship hunt, Billy's dogs had to...

    A. tree five coons.

    B. beat out four other teams of dogs.

    C. beat out two other teams of dogs.

3. When the winter storm broke out on the last night of the hunt, Billy wanted to...

    A. go back to camp so his dogs wouldn't freeze to death.

    B. keep going so his dogs could tree more coons.

    C. build a fire and wait for the storm to end.

4. Grandpa got lost in the winter storm because he...

    A. had tripped over a broken tree limb and injured his ankle.

    B. had gone looking for Billy's dogs alone.

    C. couldn't find the right direction in the blowing storm.

5. The judge was amazed at Billy's dogs because...

    A. they were fast runners.

    B. they were never outsmarted by a raccoon.

    C. they were unusually smart for redbone hounds.

6. When treeing their final coon, Billy's dogs spent the night running around the tree because they...

    A. didn't want the coon to escape.

    B. were excited and understood what the coon meant to Billy.

    C. would have frozen to death if they hadn't kept moving.

7. After Billy showed Mama the gold cup and gave her the $300, she...

    A. brought the dogs into the house for a special meal.

    B. knelt on her knees in prayer by the doghouse.

    C. wanted to show the gold cup to Grandmother.

8. Old Dan wouldn't leave the tree where the mountain lion was perched because...

    A. hunting was bred into him.

    B. he knew the mountain lion would attack if he turned away.

    C. he thought he had treed a raccoon.

9. Billy helped his dogs in their fight with the mountain lion by...

    A. clubbing it with a heavy tree limb.

    B. shooting at it with his rifle.

    C. hacking at it with his ax.

10. The legend of the red fern says the seeds of the fern were planted by...

    A. an Indian hunter.

    B. an angel.

    C. God.

Vocabulary

Directions:

Fill in the blank with

the correct word.

faltered	awed	probed
trudged	allotted	avail
defiant	predatory	verge
	lithe	

1. _____   searched

2. _____   full of boldness; challenging

3. _____   wavered; lost confidence; became unsteady

4. _____   divided up or distributed by lot

5. _____   advantage; use or help

6. _____   easily bent; flexible; limber

7. _____   wearily walked or tramped

8. _____   the edge, brink, or margin of something

9. _____   preying on another animal

10. _____   influenced by fear or respect

Essay Questions

Directions:

Answer in complete

sentences.

1. During the championship hunt, the other teams were rooting for Billy's dogs. Why do you think they wanted Billy to win?

   _____

   _____

   _____

   _____

2. When Billy's mother received the $300 prize money, she knew that her prayers had been answered. What had Mama prayed for?

   _____

   _____

   _____

   _____

3. The judges were amazed by Billy's dogs. Why do you suppose Billy's dogs were so much smarter than the average redbone hounds?

   _____

   _____

   _____

Chapter Title _____   Name _____

Chapter Summary: _____

_____

_____

_____

_____

_____

_____

_____

_____

_____

_____

_____

_____

_____

_____

_____

Chapter Vocabulary:

1. _____

_____

_____

2. _____

_____

_____

3. _____

_____

_____

4. _____

_____

_____

NAME: _____

Where the Red Fern Grows

Skill Page: Setting of *Red Fern*. Page 10.

Skill Page: Elements of a Narrative. Page 16.

Main Character

A. Billy is a country boy whose poor family barely makes a living from farming.

B. Billy desperately wants two coon hunting dogs—something his poor family cannot afford to give him.

C. Billy shows grit and determination by resolving to work and save for his pups himself.

Setting

A. **Where:** The story takes place in the foothils of the rugged Oklahoma Ozark Mountains.

B. **When:** The story takes place sometime in the early 1900s. (Inference)

Plot

A. Billy is heartbroken when his parents tell him that they cannot afford to buy him two coon pups.

B. After initially becoming very depressed and discouraged, Billy decides to earn the money himself.

C. Billy works very hard at tough jobs (picking berries, catching and selling minnows) in order to get his pups.

D. Billy finally gets his pups, and they share many adventures together—some happy, some sad.

Accept reasonable answers.

Skill Page: Getting Organized. Page 18.

Boy Dog	Girl Dog
•Physical Characteristics	
larger	smaller
deeper red	shorter legs and body
broad, solid chest	small, delicate head
knotted, rippling muscles	
•Personality Characteristics	
bold, aggressive	timid, cautious
brave	smart

What Billy Sold	Examples of Prices
crawfish, minnows	berries—10¢ a bucket
fresh vegetables	opossum hide—15¢
blackberries, huckleberries	skunk hide—25¢

Methods Billy Used for Catching/Hunting/Picking

Caught crawfish with bare hands.

Trapped minnows with a screen-wire trap.

Trapped opossum, skunks, and rabbits with steel trap.

Picked blackberries until his feet were red and raw.

Test: Chapters 1-5. Page 19-21.

Multiple Choice

1. B	6. C
2. C	7. B
3. B	8. A
4. A	9. C
5. B	10. B

Vocabulary

1. muster	6. festered
2. ventured	7. dormant
3. amends	8. aromatic
4. winced	9. grit
5. sparsely	10. mulled

Essay Questions

1. Wilson Rawls opened with the flashback technique because he wanted to engage his reader in the excitement of the dogfight. He wanted them to keep on reading.

2. When the man saw the dogs ganging up on the old coon hound, he remembered another redbone hound that had given his life so that the man might live.

3. The marshal was referring to the fact that Billy had worked and saved for two years to buy his pups.

Accept reasonable answers.

Skill Page: Identifying Characters. Page 25.

1. Billy	9. Billy
2. Mama	10. Mama
3. Papa	11. Billy's sister
4. Papa	12. Papa
5. Billy	13. Papa
6. Grandpa	14. Billy
7. Boy in Tahlequah	15. Mama
8. Marshal	

Skill Page: Outlining. Page 29.

I.   Popularity
   A. Intelligent and adaptable
   B. Favorite of authors
   C. Appear in stories and folktales

II. Physical Appearance
   A. Black mask
       1. Across its eyes
       2. Looks like bandit
   B. Grey or brown fur
   C. Tail
       1. Bushy
       2. Ringed with black markings

III. Characteristics
   A. "Washing food"
       1. Done in captivity
       2. Makes up for "missed behavior" in wild
   B. Forepaws
       1. Five fingers
       2. Highly manipulative
   C. Eating habits
       1. Carnivores
       2. Also eat plants

IV. Habitat
   A. Woodlands—near water
   B. Open country or suburbs
   C. Range—Canada to Central America

V.   Hunting Raccoons
   A. Done at night
   B. Reasons for hunting
       1. Coonskins
       2. Damage to crops

Test: Chapters 6-10. Page 32-34.

Multiple Choice

1. C	6. C
2. A	7. B
3. B	8. C
4. C	9. B
5. A	10. A

Vocabulary

1. eerie	6. wily
2. lope	7. raved
3. resistance	8. nonchalantly
4. belligerent	9. destined
5. querying	10. limbered

Essay Questions

1. At the time that Billy began coon hunting, the price for coonskins sky-rocketed, and Billy turned all his earnings over to his father. P. 99-100.

2. While Billy was working and saving to earn the money to buy his pups, he asked his grandfather to say nothing of his plans to his father. P. 20.

    When it came time to order the pups, Billy asked his grandfather to help him with the arrangements. Grandpa rewarded Billy with a sack of candy because he was so proud of him. P. 23-24..

    Grandpa came up with a plan for trapping Billy's first coon—using a brace, a bit, some horseshoe nails, and a shiny piece of tin. P. 55-56.

    Grandpa devised a plan for keeping the raccoon treed by building a scarecrow. P. 86-88.

    Grandpa often joked with Billy. (Throughout the novel.)

    Grandpa stopped Billy from telling too many lies about coon hunting by cramming a bar of soap into Billy's pocket. P. 101.

    Accept reasonable answers.

Skill Page: Sequencing. Page 37.

Event 1:   Billy gets "dog wanting disease."

Event 2:   Billy sets steel traps.

Event 3:   Billy finds magazine.

Event 4:   Billy begins saving.

Event 5:   Billy picks up pups.

Event 6:   The marshal saves Billy.

Event 7:   Billy outsmarts mountain lion.

Event 8:   Billy chops "big tree."

Event 9:   Billy gives earnings to papa.

Event 10:   Little Ann almost freezes.

Event 11:   Grandpa brags about Billy's dogs.

Event 12:   The pritchards challenge Billy.

Skill Page: Figurative Language. Page 39.

1. —	7. simile
2. simile	8. simile
3. simile	9. simile
4. simile	10. simile
5. simile	11. simile
6. simile	

Skill Page: Cause and Effect. Page 43.

1. E	6. D
2. G	7. F
3. I	8. C
4. A	9. B
5. J	10. H

Test: Chapters 11-15. Page 44-46.

Multiple Choice

1. B	6. B
2. C	7. B
3. B	8. A
4. A	9. C
5. C	10. B

Vocabulary

1. begrudgingly	6. fleeting
2. jubilant	7. plight
3. clambered	8. leering
4. gloated	9. taut
5. rile	10. stern

Essay Questions

1. Billy might have taken a back way out of Tahlequah to avoid meeting the boys who had teased him earlier. Or he might have asked the marshal to help him get out of town.

   Billy took Old Dan and Little Ann hunting after the fierce winter storm.

   Billy accepted the Pritchard boys' challenge. He could have declined or asked his grandfather to accompany them.

2. Billy chopped down the "the big tree" by himself.

   Billy jumped into the freezing river water to save Little Ann because he didn't have time to get help.

   Billy turned over his earnings from coon hunting to his father.

   Grandpa was remorseful after Rubin's death because he had accepted the Pritchard boys' challenge.

   Billy's father didn't like leaving his pregnant wife alone while he went on the hunt.

   Grandpa wanted to get Billy's mind off Rubin's death, so he organized their entry into the coon hunt.

   Mama wanted Papa to go along on the hunt because he hadn't been away from the farm in a long time.

   Accept reasonable answers.

Skill Page: Character Development. Page 53.

Possible examples to support virtues:

Responsibility:

1. When Billy's family couldn't afford to buy him the coon pups he so desperately wanted, Billy worked to save for them himself.
2. Billy chopped down "the big tree" by himself to keep his word to his dogs.
3. When Little Ann was drowning in the freezing river, Billy jumped in to save her.
4. Billy gave his mother all the money he earned from hunting and from winning the championship. Because of Billy's earnings, the family was able to move to a better life in town.

Courage:

1. Billy remained calm when the mountain lion picked up the scent of his pups. He frightened the animal away by keeping the fire going, whooping, and throwing rocks.
2. Billy pulled his ax from Rubin's body even though the sight of it sickened him.
3. Billy rushed in to try to save his dogs by hacking away at the devil cat with his ax.

Compassion:

1. The adult Billy Colman saved the old hound from the attack by a pack of dogs.
2. The child Billy shared his candy treats with his sisters, who rarely got candy.
3. Billy had to pay his respects to Rubin by laying a wreath of flowers on his grave even though it was dangerous for him to appear on the Pritchards' property.
4. Billy did extra work for his mother when he learned that she was pregnant.

Persistence:

1. Billy kept saving his money, earning only a few cents at a time, for two years until he had collected enough to buy his pups.
2. Billy walked twenty miles alone, both ways, in order to pick up his pups from the depot.
3. Billy didn't give up chopping "the big tree" until the job was done.
4. On the last night of the championship hunt, Billy wouldn't give up hunting, even when the freezing sleet fell.

Hard Work:

1. To earn money, Billy worked at difficult jobs like catching bait for fishermen, trapping and skinning animals, and collecting berries from thorny bushes.
2. Billy spent many hours carefully training his pups to hunt.
3. Billy enjoyed helping his father in the fields.

Faith:

1. Billy always said a short but heartfelt prayer when the going got rough. Billy credited God with giving him the strength and determination to chop down "the big tree" and to help save Little Ann from drowning.
2. When Billy's prayers were answered, he always remembered to thank God.
3. After finding the red fern growing between his dogs' graves, Billy felt that God was at last giving him the strength to accept his dogs' death.

Skill Page: Plot Development. Page 56.

Name _____

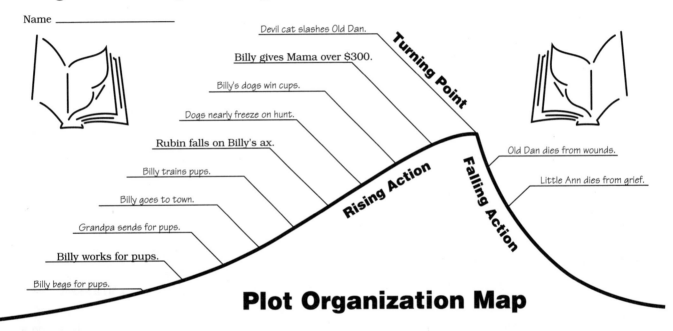

Devil cat slashes Old Dan.

Billy gives Mama over $300.

Billy's dogs win cups.

Dogs nearly freeze on hunt.

Rubin falls on Billy's ax.

Billy trains pups.

Billy goes to town.

Grandpa sends for pups.

Billy works for pups.

Billy begs for pups.

Turning Point

Rising Action

Falling Action

Old Dan dies from wounds.

Little Ann dies from grief.

Plot Organization Map

Characters
Billy Colman
Papa
Mama
Grandpa
Marshal
Boys in town
Little Ann/Old Dan
Pritchards

Setting
Foothills of the Ozark Mountains in Oklahoma.

Problem
Billy Colman, son of an Ozark farmer, wants two coon pups for hunting. The only way to get the money is to earn it himself.

Resolution
Billy's earnings allow family to move to town. Billy is comforted by the legend of the red fern.

Test: Chapters 16-20. Page 59-61.

Multiple Choice

1. B	6. C
2. C	7. B
3. B	8. A
4. A	9. C
5. C	10. B

Vocabulary

1. probed	6. lithe
2. defiant	7. trudged
3. faltered	8. verge
4. allotted	9. predatory
5. avail	10. awed

Essay Questions

1. The other hunters probably saw how well trained Billy's dogs were, even though he was only a boy. They had also probably heard the story of how hard Billy had worked and saved to buy his dogs. (Inference)

2. Mama had wanted to save enough money so that her family could move to town. She didn't want her children growing up without a proper education.

3. Billy loved his dogs far more than the average hunter did, and he spent a great deal of time training them and rewarding them for doing well. Because of the unselfish love between Billy and his dogs, they were able to perform at a higher level than other hounds. (Inference)

Accept reasonable answers.